Understand LEAN in 30 Min

Reut Barak

Copyright info

Copyright © Reut Barak

Editing by JoAnn Collins

Published by New Belle Enterprises, Understand LEAN in 30 Min, Reut Barak

All rights reserved. No part of this book may be reproduced in any manner without written permission from the publisher, except in the case of quotes used in critical articles and reviews.

To the incredible James P. Womack, Daniel T. Jones, and Daniel Roos who wrote The Machine That Changed the World. *To all the workers of Amazon who implemented it, and to John Shook who helped so many companies since project NUMMI understand Lean.*

Table of Contents

The Story of Lean..6

1. A Failing Company Ready to Rise..............................8

2. A New Culture...12

Kaizen / Continuous Improvement................................19

3. The Customer Is the Boss....................................20

Customer Obsession...24

Just-in-Time Production..25

Kanban...27

4. Controlling the Supply Chain................................28

5. Show Me Your Problems.......................................32

The 5 Whys – Root-Cause Analysis...............................34

Andon..36

6. Killing Waste to Save Money.................................38

Muda / 7 Wastes..40

7. How to Trash a New Car......................................44

SMED – Quick Die Change & Formula 1............................47

8. More Lean Concepts..49

5S...50

Process Mapping..53

Gemba Walk...54

Pareto Effect..55

Six Sigma..56
About the Author...60

The Story of Lean

Toyota. A failing company, struggling with financial loss, about to fire workers.

Fast-forward to Lean: Toyota is the number-one company in the world of car manufacturing.

How did they do it? How did this one brave company face its severe circumstances and win against all odds? Grasp this story and you will be a natural at Lean.

In this book, you will learn the basics of Lean and understand Lean tools through one of the most inspiring transformation stories in business history.

You will grasp the main elements of Lean:

- Just-in-time production
- Continuous improvement
- Eliminating waste
- Lean employee culture

And learn the basic Lean tools:

- Kanban
- Kaizen
- 5 Whys
- 7 Wastes – Muda

- 5S
- SMED, or Quick Die Change (using Formula 1 as an example – no kidding)
- Andon
- Customer Obsession
- Process Mapping
- Gemba Walk
- Pareto Effect
- Six Sigma

I promise you will never look at processes around you the same way again.

1. A Failing Company Ready to Rise

"A diamond is a chunk of coal that did well under pressure." – Henry Kissenger

It is hard to believe that Toyota's story started with failure. Most people have heard about Toyota as an example of excellence in manufacturing; and its Lean methods made other companies successful, too. For example: Project NUMMI, where Toyota took a failing General Motors plant and brought it to be one of the top three production plants in the world at its time – with 80% of the workforce still being the General Motors workforce, but under Toyota management.

But that was afterwards.

Lean Manufacturing actually resulted from a desperate attempt to survive, from a necessary need to create a new system that saved the company.

Toyota started as a truck manufacturer for the Japanese military during World War II. But in 1949, a severe reduction in sales hit; there were not enough orders coming in, so there was not enough work for its people or money to pay salaries. They decided to fire workers.

The workers' union fought back. They put up a strike and the head of the company, Kiichiro Toyoda, resigned.

Toyota faced a hostile environment on eight fronts:

1. Revenue:

When Toyota saw its sales collapse towards the end of 1949, it was producing about one thousand units per month. In comparison, the big three producers in Detroit at that time made that amount in one day, and on just one of their assembly lines.

2. Cost:

Toyota did not have the capacity to mass-produce, as American competitors of the time did, so it did not have the option of cutting costs through scale in order to survive.

3. Market demand:

After the war, the Japanese market was very small but demanded a variety of vehicles. Each different car required its own setup. In comparison, American mass-producers of the time, like Ford, only produced a handful of models.

4. Workers:

Toyota had a strong union. New labor laws, installed

by the US occupation of Japan after World War II, made it difficult to fire workers. Workers also had other good companies to choose from, so expectations from the workplace were high.

5. Finance - banks would not loan:

On top of its other financial difficulties, Toyota's bankers refused to issue new loans to the company.

6. Technology:

Due to its financial difficulties, Toyota could not afford to purchase Western machinery and technologies to match its foreign competitors who had mass-production equipment.

7. Competition:

Foreign motor producers were ready to enter Japan. These companies could successfully defend their own markets against Japanese exports. Toyota and the rest of the Japanese market had to deal with this cut-throat playing ground.

8. Government Pressure:

To top it all, the Japanese government was putting

pressure on smaller manufacturers. It was trying to design a more concentrated market by merging car producers, to create larger companies that could compete in the American market.

Couldn't be worse!

What Toyota invented to survive not only saved the company, but made it the best car producer in the world of its time, and its new production system dominated the market.

2. A New Culture

"No one can whistle a symphony. It takes a whole orchestra to play it." – Halford E. Luccock

The new Toyota Production System (TPS), now known as Lean Manufacturing, was created in 1950 by industrialist Eiji Toyoda, who visited the Ford River Rouge Plant in Detroit, and engineer Taiichi Ohno.

They did it through cultural change. This cultural element of Lean is the hardest to understand for companies looking to implement the system today. It is too different from what they know.

Let's walk into a "normal" company for a couple minutes. For one, it is rare to find employees who have been there for a long time, especially not on the shop floor. The "little people" – those who do the actual job and know the process best – are the least paid, because salaries are based on job title to encourage new managers from other companies to enter leadership roles. The workforce has limited time contracts and is easy to fire and replace. The emphasis is on doing your own job, as quickly as possible and in isolation. Expertise is not valued – it will not raise anyone's salary.

When there are peaks, teams are expected to work overtime, or hire temporary staff, and departments compete on budgets.

Most employees and managers are focused on displaying an all-is-good-here workplace. Nobody wants to be blamed when there is a problem, so issues are generally hidden or addressed with discretion. Specialists and consultants are brought in to make changes when problems occur or accumulate, usually resulting in cuts and layoffs.

Supplier contracts are based on lowest bids, or mass delivery of inventory, and contracts are renewed based on the best new bid. Competition between suppliers is high.

Sound familiar?

Now, let's walk into a strange new world. Here are the eight main elements of the cultural change of Toyota:

1. Workers with lifetime contracts:

Toyota's workers were given new contracts that ensured lifetime employment. They were also allowed to use the company's facilities and recreation for their entire lives. This commitment worked for both parties: Toyota was now sure to have a skilled workforce, experienced in the company's ways and culture.

2. Payment by seniority:

Salaries were based on seniority acquired over time, and not on job titles. This, too, ensured a skilled workforce. Over the years, people got paid more for doing the same job, so leaving for another company was an unattractive option – it meant starting from the bottom again. Workers also got to share in Toyota's successes in the form of bonuses.

3. Empowerment:

In traditional mass production, the shop-floor workers were given the least power over processes. But production was where value was added – where the next product was being built.

In TPS, workers had full control over production and maximum power was transferred to those who "do the job." They were divided into teams, and team leaders worked actively with their subordinates as part of the group. They shared all the tasks, including cleaning, problem solving, and improvement suggestion. The only difference between team leaders and their subordinates was that they had more experience.

The team did its own repairs and invented improvements to the system – a process known as Continuous Improvement, or Kaizen. Skilled employees were valued and no external experts were needed to make changes to the work.

4. Cross-department help:

If someone was sick or absent, employees from a different department pitched in. They also helped when another department had peak time and needed more staffing.

Workspace barriers were physically removed: employees worked in small spaces and could see each other's processes to align efforts. When something went wrong, any employee who knew how to fix it lent a hand, even if they were from another team or department. There was an understanding that when people worked in isolation, each doing their own part, the whole system would lose. But when everyone worked together, and each person could see their contribution to the whole, the system benefited.

To enable all of this, workers were cross-trained. For example: as part of engineer training, employees had to work a few months in the marketing department. Each employee, including senior management, had to spend one month a year in a different functional area. When MIT came to research Lean production at Honda – a company that adopted TPS – a senior director was unavailable for interviews because he was busy assembling cars. You can read about it in the book, *The*

Machine that Changed the World.

Today at Amazon, a leading Lean company, during peak season, analysts and managers leave their desks to join shop floor in packaging and to take on delivery shifts.

5. Helping your suppliers:

Toyota also sent its employees to suppliers when they had an overload of work. It sent its managers to assist with suppliers' improvement efforts. Profits were shared, and Toyota bought supplier stocks and provided banking for suppliers (more on supplier relationships in chapter 4). Contracts were long term and suppliers had associations where information was shared and improvements were discussed.

6. Never hiding your problems:

Due to its financial constraints, Toyota could not afford to waste materials on defected units. It was, therefore, essential to create a culture where problems were exposed and addressed. When a problem occurred, workers were encouraged to stop production immediately, and find the root cause to eliminate the chance that the problem would ever recur (more on problem solving in chapter 5 and eliminating waste in chapter 6).

7. Loving your customer:

Putting people's needs first was part of how Toyota treated customers. Salespeople would lend the customer a car while their cars were being repaired and kept in constant touch with the family (more on customer care in the next chapter). Toyota also fixed cars for free even after the warranty was over.

8. The Shusha

When designing a new car, the lead engineer, called the Shusha, was in charge and given direct power (more on the new design process in chapter 7). The Shusha was loaned workers from across the company and had power over their departments – this included having staff from Toyota's sales force on the design team to ensure new cars matched customer needs. Conflicts were raised early in the process to insure commitment and smooth production afterwards.

It seems that the original unionized battle to block layoffs proved to be a blessing in disguise. It created a new culture of partnerships.

Perhaps this is the right place to mention that the core of Lean is NEVER about reducing headcount. In companies where this approach is used, Lean practitioners soon find that their work is met with resistance and austerity. In successful projects, where results last and the organization does not revert to its old ways, there are no layoffs. Instead, people whose roles are no longer needed, are offered new jobs within the changing organization.

In the next chapters you will learn more about the culture of Lean and its process of excellence like production on demand to reduce waste, and production in small batches to meet a variety of customer needs.

We have mentioned Continuous Improvement in this chapter. Let's have a closer look at this concept.

Kaizen / Continuous Improvement

What is Kaizen?

Kaizen is the Lean term for Continuous Improvement, the process through which problems are constantly exposed and fixed at the core so that they do not recur.

Translation from Japanese:

Kaizen means change for the better.

How is it used?

In a Lean culture, workers are encouraged to report problems as they surface and participate in researching the root cause of the problem to eliminate any recurrence. As a result, processes are quicker, defects are eliminated, and the system benefits from overall efficiency and cost-cuts.

3. The Customer Is the Boss

"There is only one boss. The customer. And he can fire everybody in the company from the chairman on down, simply by spending his money somewhere else." – Sam Walton

A large part of the financial success of TPS over the traditional mass production of its time, was embedding change throughout the value chain: starting with supply and going all the way to distribution. We will cover distribution and Toyota's customers in this chapter and supply in the next one.

In traditional mass production, manufacturers sold cars to dealers, who displayed them in large showrooms. The dealer ordered stock based on sales forecasts without sharing this information with the manufacturer, who then ordered parts and produced the finished products. Salespeople were incentivized based on number of cars sold rather than building long-term relationships with customers, and were trained in sales and not in car mechanics. Unwanted stock that was difficult to market was price-reduced and eventually sold at a discount.

Toyota could not afford to produce cars that would not sell or sell at a discount, so it had to reinvent its distribution approach.

1. The car comes to the customer:

Instead of going to a dealership to buy a car, Toyota's customers were visited at home by its salespeople. Sales teams had seven to eight members, and each team member visited homes periodically. When a car was needed, they suggested a suitable model, brought it on their next visit and, if the customer was satisfied, ordered it along with car insurance. Once the vehicle was ready, they delivered it personally and took care of the trade-in of the old car.

2. Going the extra mile:

If a customer's car needed repair, Toyota lent the customer a car during that time. It fixed cars for free after warranty was over, dealt with insurance claims, and kept in constant touch with the family, sending cards for birthdays and funerals.

3. Keeping a customer database:

Toyota's salespeople collected customer information:

- How many cars the family owned.
- How many kids of a driving age were in the

family and when they would need their first car.

- When the family would need a new car.
- When the family would need to repurchase (this happened every six years in Japan at the time, due to strict regulations requiring pricy part changes after the car had been in service for a few years).

When sales were low, Toyota created new demand by targeting customers who were suitable for the cars that Toyota could produce at the time.

4. Making only cars that would sell:

Salespeople were loaned to Toyota's design teams, to produce the best cars, based on customer needs and the information collected when they visited homes. Toyota made only the cars that its customers wanted and nothing else, so it did not produce cars that would not sell or sell at a discount. The focus was to make a variety of cars with superior reliability for the driver.

5. Repairs facility instead of a large dealership:

Toyota dealerships were small, with only three to four models, to reduce inventory waste. In fact, the entire distribution chain did not hold more than 21 days of finished goods. Instead of displaying cars, the space was used as a repair area, which was a source of income for the dealership.

6. Owning distribution channels:

Toyota owned distribution channels, each with its own market segment. The channel sold through dealer firms, who were 20% owned by Toyota and their staff was trained by Toyota as well. They, too, had regular problem-solving sessions.

It is important to note that, sadly, this distribution system was used by Toyota only in Japan; in other parts of the world Toyota used traditional dealers.

Let's look at Lean concepts that relate to this chapter.

Customer Obsession

What is Customer Obsession?

It is the understanding that the very worst scenario for a business is losing its customers and everything must be done to keep customers happy and coming back. It is a modern business concept, taken from Lean production.

How is it used?

Let's use the case of Amazon to illustrate this concept. One of the first things that Jeff Bezos said to his staff when starting Amazon was not to focus on the competition because the competition was not paying them, and instead to focus on the customer because that was where the money came from. Today, Amazon is known for accepting returned products without asking questions, even in the case of user error or misuse, or after warranty has passed, and with staff ready to solve problems on the phone 24 hours a day for free. This creates the necessary confidence in the customer to make online purchases and prefer Amazon to other retailers.

Just-in-Time Production

What is Just in Time?

The book, *Lean Lexicon*, defines Just in Time as "a system of production that makes and delivers just what is needed, just when it is needed." The heart of Lean is doing only what is valuable.

How is it used?

Just in Time means starting from demand and producing in order to meet it. But it goes far beyond just making the right products. It is the fundamental understanding that there is no virtue in producing more items, more parts, or more work than that for which the customer is going to pay. It is like reversing the thought process of work and starting from the end:

- When is a new car needed?
- What are the parts that must be assembled?
- What work is needed to assemble these parts?

On the production line, it means making parts only when they are needed, using Kanbans (see next concept).

Throughout the company, this also means eliminating unnecessary meetings, reports, statistical analyses that are not contributing to improvement, webinars, internal politics – anything that stops the workers from performing the actual job, which is to make what the customer buys. An Amazon manager once told me that his team did not use PowerPoint slides in their meetings, because "making them is a waste of time, and the customer doesn't value that we use them."

The illusion of automation:

In mass production, there was often a thought that automation was the secret to efficiency. Unfortunately, automation meant more machinery and more machine breakdowns. It also meant that workers were not as skilled as those who were part of Lean production. During the time of the MIT research of Lean production (see the book, *The Machine That Changed the World*), the most efficient manufacturing plant in the world was a Japanese plant that was the least automated.

Kanban

What is Kanban?

Kanban is a scheduling tool for manufacturing, used to send a signal to either start production of a part or commence a process.

Translation from Japanese:

Kanban means sign or signboard.

How is it used?

The best known example of the use of Kanban is Kanban cards that are sent to the manufacturing team to signal that manufacturing should start. Manufacturing only starts when the Kanban arrives. The card will include:

- A description of the part that needs to be made
- Technical information about the part
- Quantity
- Location of storage
- The manufacturing process needed.

4. Controlling the Supply Chain

"Shake the hand that feeds you." – Michael Pollan

In traditional mass production, there was little collaboration between assemblers and their suppliers. Once a part was needed, the company collected bids, then negotiated with the suppliers it chose. The most important aspect of the relationship with suppliers was lowering the cost. Therefore, the larger the supplier and the more they used economies of scale, the better their bargaining power.

Contracts were short, up to one year, and the pressure on cost reduction created fierce competition between suppliers. Manufacturers made this competition worse: After their chosen suppliers had completed the lengthy process of creating production-ready designs, they sent the final ones to new suppliers to try and get lower prices. As a result, suppliers kept their manufacturing processes as discreet as possible, sharing as little information as possible with car producers, and avoiding collaborations with other suppliers.

Different suppliers were needed to produce all the individual components of a car, which meant that at the end of the process parts could arrive from various companies and not fit together. Ready parts also required error-fixing and debugging.

Instead of dealing with many suppliers for all the components required, Toyota created a Tier System: It would deal with first-tier suppliers who produced the full parts (e.g., wheels), and the first-tier suppliers, in turn, used second-tier suppliers to produce smaller components (e.g., screws).

Full collaboration between first-tier and second-tier suppliers meant that all components matched the parts' designs. This also reduced the number of suppliers Toyota had to deal with to about one fifth of the traditional mass-production system, so less workforce was needed to deal with suppliers.

Suppliers were chosen based on past relationships, not bids, and contracts were long term. Failure to deliver meant reduction of business until the supplier mended its problems. Contracts were drawn based on the target market price of the finished car, and deciding how to ensure enough profit to both the manufacturer and the suppliers. Toyota held shares in its suppliers' companies, and also served them as a bank, giving them loans so they could purchase materials to produce parts. There were no exclusivity clauses in the contracts, and suppliers were encouraged to also produce parts for other companies at a higher profit.

During the manufacturing process, manufacturers and

suppliers collaborated on reducing wastes and inefficiencies to bring down costs. Toyota would send its managers to assist with the suppliers' improvement efforts and also sent workers when the suppliers had an overload of work. Improvements were openly discussed and the focus was on quality, not on price. Continuous Improvement meant lower running costs and enabled cutting prices during market slumps. Suppliers were grouped into supplier associations, where improvements and market opportunities were shared.

Parts were delivered to the assembly line, just when Toyota needed them, with transportation carts going back and forth, to avoid piling inventories at both the supplier and producer plants.

Let's recap: Traditional Mass Production vs. Lean:

- Instead of: little collaboration between the assemblers and their suppliers – full collaboration that includes holding shares, banking, and sending workers to suppliers.
- Instead of: dealing with many suppliers for all the parts (e.g., suppliers for the wheel parts) – dealing with a few suppliers for one tier of parts (e.g., suppliers for whole wheels).
- Instead of: choosing suppliers based on collecting bids, then negotiating – choosing

suppliers based on past relationships.

- Instead of: focusing on lowering the cost – focusing on quality and sharing the profits.
- Instead of: short contracts – long term contracts and relationship building.
- Instead of: fierce competition between suppliers – suppliers have associations where improvements are discussed to increase quality.
- Instead of: not knowing how the suppliers' manufacturing processes work because it is kept discreet – sending managers to assist with the suppliers with improvement efforts.

The following diagram summarizes Toyota's relationship across the value chain:

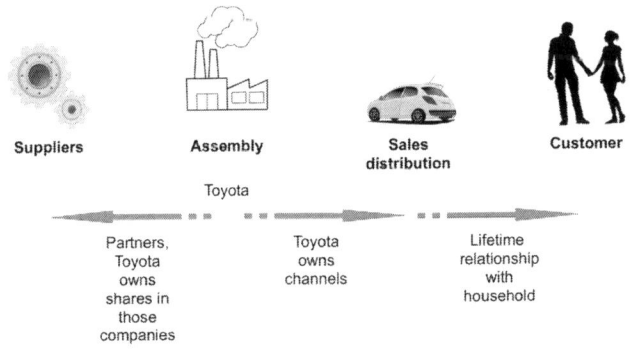

This concludes the information on Toyota's culture. In the next two chapters we will look at its operational excellence.

5. Show Me Your Problems

"No problem is a problem" – John Shook, Toyota Manager, Project NUMMI

So far, we have looked at the failure story and severe conditions that led Toyota to create Lean Manufacturing and dominate its market from a cultural perspective. In this chapter, we will look at the way it achieved superior manufacturing quality.

In many working cultures today, problems are hushed and hidden. Employees tend to avoid pointing out issues for many reasons:

- Fear they might eventually get blamed
- Fear of overstepping authority
- Fear that pointing out a flaw is bad manners
- Fear of being the bearer of bad news
- Fear of rocking the boat

Mass production focused on keeping the assembly line going and moving the items through as fast as possible. If an error occurred, it continued down the line, resulting in rework or scrapping of parts and even assembled cars.

Due to its financial constraints, Toyota could not afford to throw away material or waste money on rework. So it was essential to create a culture where problems were exposed and addressed.

This meant stopping production immediately when a problem was discovered. A new and innovative idea!

Workers had a mechanism that stopped the line, known as the Andon cord. Once production stopped, the team either solved the problem themselves or asked for assistance. Defects were fixed on the spot, or the part was taken to a special station to investigate why the damage occurred and identify the source of the problem. A new process was then introduced that was fail-safe and the problem never recurred.

It was hard at first. Assembly lines stopped constantly. But over time, production had reached such a level of being error-free, that the lines moved swiftly, no more rework was needed, and there was no waste of time or space for reworking parts. This is the true result of Continuous Improvement.

To stop problems from recurring, Toyota used the 5 - Whys method. Let's have a closer look at this concept and the Andon.

The 5 Whys – Root-Cause Analysis

What is 5 Whys?

Five Whys is a methodology used to identify the root cause of a problem by asking the question "Why" five times to reveal the different layers of the situation.

How is it used?

Jeff Bezos, CEO of Amazon, once described a day when he was sweeping dust on the floor of a warehouse, then the Lean Japanese expert told him to focus more on what was creating dust in the first place.

This is an example of identifying root cause.

Five Whys is the most efficient form of root-cause analysis. It ensures a thorough investigation of a problem and then provides a sustainable solution that eliminates any recurrence. Its importance lies in the fact that if the true cause of a problem is not identified, the wrong solution might be applied, wasting money and resources, and creating inefficient processes.

Here is an easy example from everyday life:

Problem: I arrived home late.

1. Why? I missed the train.

2. Why? I did not arrive at the platform on time.

3. Why? I was delayed at the ticket office.

4. Why? There was a large line at the ticket office.

5. Why? There was a football match and many people wanted to purchase tickets today.

Solution: Buy tickets in advance, especially on days that have events that might cause congestion in the ticket office. This will ensure the problem never recurs.

Andon

What is Andon?

Andon is a tool that shows workers the overview of a process and highlights problems (e.g., shows which assembly station has an issue).

Translation from Japanese:

Andon means lamp.

How is it used?

The Andon Cord was a rope used to stop the assembly line when problems occurred. It could be used by any worker – any employee could stop production. The Andon system then showed everyone which workstation had a problem. Here is an example from Toyota Motomachi:

1. A team member recognizes a defective part.
2. The team member pulls the Andon cord.
3. The board above the production line will show a yellow light at the numbered workstation with the problem.
4. A chime sounds to let everyone know of the incident.

5. The team leader goes to the affected workstation to help solve the problem.

6. The team leader pulls the Andon cord to turn off the light on the board if the problem is solved. If the problem cannot be solved, the production line will stop and the Andon will light the problematic workstation in red, calling other workers to step in and help.

The Andon allows everyone in the production line to know, at a glance, the state of all the workstations.

6. Killing Waste to Save Money

"Mass production is designed with buffers everywhere—extra inventory, extra space, extra workers—in order to make it function." – James P. Womack, Daniel T. Jones & Daniel Roos, The Machine That Changed the World

In the heart of Lean manufacturing lie two concepts:

- Stopping production to solve problems – we discussed this in the previous chapter.
- Eliminating waste.

Waste is one of the highest costs to a company.

It comes in seven forms: inventory, transportation, over-production, over-processing, defects, waiting, and motion. All of these waste money and employee time.

Getting rid of inventory:

We will start by introducing the idea that inventory is essentially bad for production. UPS corporate strategist Alan Amling, once stated that "inventory is the devil," because it adds to losses.

Not only does inventory substantially increase the costs of space and rental, it hides where there is an ongoing issue in the system. One of Toyota's revolutions was to eliminate inventory as far as possible in order to expose which step of the assembly process was the slowest: that step required more inventory after it to keep smooth production. That place was the bottleneck – without inventory, the next step in the process was stuck waiting for work. This was where improvements were needed.

In TPS, only one hour's worth of inventory was traditionally kept at workstations.

Just-in-Time production and Kanbans also helped keep inventory at its minimum, as no unnecessary parts were produced. Workers were not busy without cause and could lend a hand to other areas of the business.

These efforts were aligned with Toyota's suppliers: a container arrived from the supplier straight to the assembly line a few times a day and returned empty to gather more parts. Inventory did not pile up at assembly or the suppliers' facilities, and fewer transportation vehicles were needed.

Let's have a further look at inventory and the rest of the seven wastes by studying the Lean concept of Muda.

Muda / 7 Wastes

What is Muda?

Muda is a work that consumes resources and time and does not create value.

Translation from Japanese:

Muda means waste.

How is it used?

There are seven wastes in Lean production. All of them are costly as they waste resources, time, space, employee hours, and materials.

1. Inventory:

    - It wastes: Space and materials.

    - An easy example: Milk piling up and going out of date in a cake factory, because of a slow and inefficient workspace that is not moving fast enough further down the line.

    - How it damages profit: The company loses money by paying for inventory storage – space is pricey, and in our example the cost of electricity to keep milk cool is high. Materials are costly and deteriorate over time, in which case more money is spent to get new materials.

2. Waiting:

- It wastes: Time and employee hours.

- An easy example: Workers waiting by a broken machine for technical support to arrive.

- How it damages profit: The company loses money because employees are idle while waiting. The company might miss deadlines as a result, lose clients, and have to issue refunds. To catch up and meet deadlines, it must now hire more staff or pay high overtime salaries.

3. Transportation:

- It wastes: Time and employee hours.

- An easy example: Moving finished goods to a warehouse for storage when direct delivery to customers was possible.

- How it damages profit: The company loses money by paying more for unnecessary movement of parts and for transportation costs. In this case, there are also storage costs.

4. Defects:

- It wastes: Time, employee hours, and materials.
- An easy example: Products with flaws that must be fixed in order to sell them.
- How it damages profit: The company loses money by paying for rework.

5. Over-production:

- It wastes: Time, space, employee hours, and materials.
- An easy example: A company producing more finished goods than it knows it can sell.
- How it damages profit: The company loses money by potentially producing too much of the wrong product – an investment it cannot return.

6. Over-processing:

- It wastes: Time, space, employee hours, and materials.
- An easy example: Engaging in internal research that makes a department look good, but does not help the company.

- How it damages profit: The company loses money by paying for manpower hours, materials, and work that is not needed.

7. Motion:

- It wastes: Time, space, and employee hours.
- An easy example: People moving from office to office to collect documents that could be sent through internal mail.
- How it damages profit: The company loses money by paying for unnecessary activities that waste employer time.

7. How to Trash a New Car

*"Have Backbone; Disagree and Commit." –
Jeff Bezos & Amazon leadership principles*

In traditional mass production, designing a new car took five to seven years. It consisted of assigning a lead engineer and providing them with a budget and a team. The engineer's power was limited and their success depended on coordinating the efforts and wants of the different departments, and convincing these departments to remain within the time and budget that was agreed upon. Designs were based on research, sales patterns, and customer surveys, and any changes in the market during this lengthy time period meant redesigns and waste. The number of people and the budget increased towards the end of the process to resolve problems and complete the designs.

The Shusha:

In Lean production, the process was led by an engineer with direct power who was a boss-leader, known as Shusha. The engineer was given workers from the departments they had to work with, so they had direct power in those departments. The workers still belonged to the departments and returned to them afterwards. Their promotion depended on the quality of their work with the Shusha. New products were later known by their Shusha name.

Commitment was made at the beginning with team members signing a pledge to do what the team agreed upon. Two things happened as a result:

- The team's commitment forced collaboration across departments.
- Conflicts surfaced early on and were resolved, so the process was smooth afterwards and there were no surprises at the end. This also saved money: budget reduced towards the end of the project and team members who were no longer needed moved to other roles.

Sales force members were also loaned to the Shusha's team, and designs were based on the information gathered from the customer database.

Development was tiered: one team worked on the basic car, and others worked on variations.

The whole process was completed within four years. This was partly due to existing collaborations between departments: each step already knew how to make parts so that the next step could use them. There was less need for detailed component instructions. The same was true for the knowledge gained from partnership with suppliers: a Lean system required only

30% detailed engineering of parts compared to 81% in traditional mass production (see: *The Machine That Changed the World*).

Speaking of needing a new car...

In the first chapter, we mentioned the Japanese market wanted a variety of models, but how could a smaller manufacturer without economies of scale meet such a demand?

Toyota did this by inventing a Quick Die Change system. Let's have a closer look.

SMED – Quick Die Change & Formula 1

What is SMED?

SMED or Single-Minute Exchange of Die, is a method of a quick change of machinery between producing one product to producing the next.

What does it mean?

Change of Die refers not only to changing a die but to changing the different cutting and shaping tools needed to produce a different car.

How is it used?

This is best explained using the example of a Formula 1 pit stop. In the 50s, changing the wheels of a Formula 1 car took over a minute and the engineer who did it, one step at a time, was glorified. Now, a trained team with standardized tools replaces all four wheels in less than three seconds.

Toyota invented Quick Die Change in order to produce different models of cars easily. It was a great achievement: machinery change time went down from over a day to under ten minutes. Not only did this enable producing a variety of cars in small batches to target different customers, it also reduced defects because mistakes in smaller batches were easier to detect.

The process had two steps:

1. Standardizing machinery measurements so that the change could happen accurately, without human adjustment.
2. Preparing the environment so that the new die was ready to be placed while the old one was being removed.

8. More Lean Concepts

You mastered the basics of Lean once you understood the Toyota story. But there are a few more concepts that could prove great tools in your journey to cultural excellence and production efficiency.

These are:

- 5S
- Process Mapping
- Gemba Walk
- Pareto Effect
- Six Sigma

5S

What is 5S?

The 5S is a process that creates an efficient work environment from both visual and practical perspectives.

The 5S's are: Sort, Straighten, Shine, Standardize, and Sustain – or the Japanese equivalent – Seiri, Seiton, Seiso, Seiketsu, and Shitsuke.

How is it used?

To explain 5S, we will use the Konmari method for efficiently arranging your house:

1. Sort:

- Keep only what is really wanted and get rid of what you do not need.
- Benefit: eliminates any messy clutter that stops you from finding what you want when you need it.
- For example: donate old books and clothing.
- In a company: clutter and mess prevent employees from doing their job efficiently.

2. Straighten:

- Put everything in the right place, visible and easy to reach.

- Benefit: eliminates motion waste, which happens when you have trouble getting to what you need – like not putting your phone charger in a drawer full of entangled electric wires, and then having to wrestle with the wires when you need to charge your phone.

- For example: place items in drawers in a way that makes it easy to see their contents in a glimpse of an eye.

- In a company: motion waste forces employees to have to reach for tools that are not close by, or are difficult to find.

3. Shine:

- Cleaning.

- Benefit: a tidy environment prevents health hazards like mold and dust accumulation, as well as damage to furniture, electric items, and clothing.

- For example: vacuuming.

- In a company: a tidy environment makes it

easy to notice any dangerous leaks, machine damages or other obstacles.

4+5. Standardize and Sustain:

- Create a system that retains all the effort achieved.
- Benefit: prevents relapse.
- For example: tell everyone where everything is in the new order, and teach them to keep it that way.
- In a company: ensures everyone is familiar with the new way of doing things so there will not be a need to redo the previous steps.

Process Mapping

What is Process Mapping?

Process Mapping is a technique that creates a flowchart to track an entire process and highlight any inefficiency and waste.

How is it used?

Process mapping creates a flowchart that summarizes every step of the production process, usually with its materials, length, and product.

A simplified example: Morning routine process mapping could result in the following flowchart. A few common symbols here: Circle for start, diamond for decision, and rectangles for steps in the process.

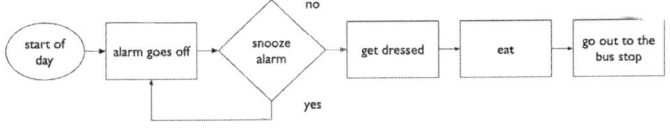

In a more detailed flowchart, it is easy to identify the "weakest link" or bottleneck of the process – the longest or most inefficient part. Improving it speeds the entire process.

Gemba Walk

What is a Gemba Walk?

A Gemba Walk is a management practice of going to the place where the work happens and examining it.

Translation from Japanese:

Gemba means actual place.

How is it used?

Gemba allows decision makers to observe how products are made, the people and machines involved, and any inefficiencies within the process. Without it, all solutions or improvement efforts would be too theoretical to be successful.

Pareto Effect

What is Pareto Effect?

Pareto is a principle that states that 80% of the output is caused by 20% of the input. It is named after Italian economist Vilfredo Pareto.

How is it used?

Pareto effect is a way to focus on the main cause, and measure its effects. For example: "20% of the donors of a charity make 80% of the donations."

Six Sigma

It is impossible to write a book on Lean without touching on Six Sigma (after all, we now call it "Lean Six Sigma"). I promise to keep this chapter as qualitative and easy-to-read as possible using a cucumber cutting example.

What is Six Sigma?

Sigma is a letter in the Greek alphabet: *σ*. In 1986 Motorola invented methods to measure variation within a system. Some used the mathematical formula for standard deviation, symbolized by sigma.

How is it used?

Okay, let's cut some cucumbers: If you try to cut 1 cm cucumber slices, the slices will be slightly larger or smaller than 1 cm, no matter how accurate your knife.

No big deal. It is just cucumbers. What is a little bit of variation in size, right? But what if instead, you were cutting diamonds, for laser-surgery machines?

Six Sigma methods test our variation by:

- Measuring how spread out our cucumber sizes are – this is called distribution of data points.
- Testing that over 99.99% are around 1 cm long – and therefore deemed defect-free.

Below is a simplified chart: We have cut 11 slices of cucumber and plotted their sizes. Let's also assume that we already ran all the six sigma calculations and we know that we can accept all slices that are between 0.7 cm and 1.3 cm.

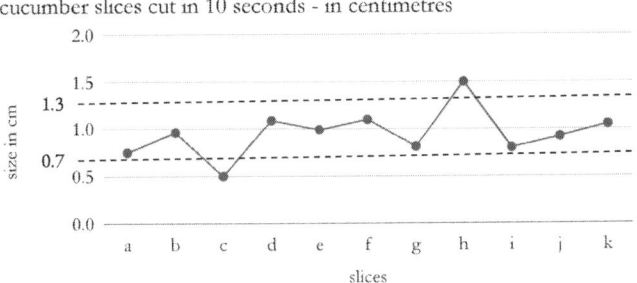

As you can see, no two slices were the same size, though some were very similar (like 'a' and 'i', or 'd' and 'f'). We have two types of variations:

1. Slices c and h are outside our range. They are called special-cause variation.

2. The other slices also have variations, but this is a natural part of any process. They are called common-cause variation or intrinsic noise.

But where does the name "Six Sigma" come from?

"Sigma", or σ, comes from the statistical standard deviation formula. It is a term that means quality – a project that has Six Sigma level has less than 3.4 defects per million.

Let's conclude with looking at the formula of Sigma – it is the formula for standard deviation.

When we say something deviates, we mean it strays from where we think it should go, like a ship that moves away from its planned course.

Let's assume our average cucumber slice is 1.0 cm thick. We want to know how much our entire cutting deviated from this average. How much "mistake" in cutting are we making?

$$\sigma = \sqrt{\frac{\Sigma(x_i - \mu)^2}{n}}$$

We have 11 slices of cucumber.

Each slice has a different thickness: 0.8 cm, 1.0 cm, 0.5 cm, etc. These are called "data points." Data points are x_i.

For simplicity, let's assume our average slice is 1.0 cm thick. Average is all the slices divided by the total: 0.8+1.0+0.5 etc. divided by 11. Average is μ.

How much thicker or thinner are our slices from 1.0 cm? To avoid any negative numbers we will square that: $(0.8 - 1.0)^2$, $(1.0 - 1.0)^2$, $(0.5 - 1.0)^2$, etc. This is $(x_i - \mu)^2$.

We want the whole deviation, so we will need to first sum it up: $(0.8 - 1.0)^2+(1.0 - 1.0)^2+(0.5 - 1.0)^2$ etc. Sum is Σ.

And then divide by 11 to average it out. 11 is our "population size." Population size is n.

Finally, we must use the root function, $\sqrt{}$, since we did a square before.

Our result is our standard deviation. Let's assume it is 0.1 cm. This means our cucumbers are on average 0.1 cm larger or smaller than 1 cm. This is also called "sigma."

About the Author

The boring bit:

Reut Barak-Smith started her career as an air-force business analyst. She holds an MBA from the University of Oxford and worked as a Project Manager in the fields of manufacturing, finance, and energy, with projects up to a value of $500m. Passing both her Lean Six Sigma Green Belt and Black Belt exams above 90%, she also holds a Prince2 Practitioner, Scrum Master, Level3 Investment Operations Certificate (IOC), EIMA Practitioner and an ISEB Practitioner.

The exciting bit:

Incidentally, she also has a bachelor's degree in opera singing, and an adventurous love for hiking in the highlands. She's passionate about her self-publishing business and her books in both fantasy fiction and funny fairytales, and her raw vegan cookbooks and YouTube channel. She likes to play Mozart concertos to her toddler and play board games with her husband.

Want to know more? Check her out and see her other books now on: www.reutbarak.com/books.

Made in the USA
Columbia, SC
03 November 2023